UNVEILING
CICADA 3301
An Internet Mystery

By

Bhavesh Tekwani

Unveiling Cicada 3301

An Internet Mystery

BHAVESH TEKWANI

CENTRA PUBLISHING

AUTHOR

BHAVESH TEKWANI

Centra Publishing © 2019

CONTENTS

LEGAL NOTES

INTRODUCTION

Cicada 3301, many have heard of it, and the few who haven't will eventually learn about the secret group that has turned heads. With puzzles, cryptic books, and a scavenger hunt around the world, this secret cult goes the extra mile.

Cicada 3301 is a nickname given to an organization that on three occasions has posted a set of puzzles to recruit codebreakers from the public.

Why? Although that's a very good question, even conspiracy theorists are having a hard time with this one.
We do know that this group seeks intelligent individuals to recruit. Whether Cicada 3301 is a government ploy to hire future employees on the side or some kids trolling, the puzzles certainly

stump most people and adding a book with a secret language to decrypt doesn't make it better.

What is Cicada?
Cicadas are insects, best known for the songs sung by most, but not all. Once the cicada hatches from the egg it will begin to feed on the tree fluids. At this point, it looks like a termite or small white ant. Once the young cicada is ready, it crawls from the groove and falls to the ground where it will dig until it finds roots to feed on. It will typically start with smaller grassroots and work its way up to the roots of its host tree. The cicada will stay underground from 2 to 17 years depending on the species. Cicadas are active underground, tunneling, and feeding, and not sleeping or hibernating as commonly thought.
After the long 2 to 17 years, cicadas emerge from the ground as nymphs. Nymphs climb the nearest available tree and begin to shed their nymph exoskeleton. Free of their old skin, their wings will inflate with fluid and their adult skin will harden.

Cicada 3301 has been called "the most elaborate and mysterious puzzle of the internet age." The Washington Post ranked it as one of the "Top 5 eeriest, unsolved mysteries of the internet." Seven years after the elaborate cryptographic puzzle contest first launched, it still seems that no one except the person(s) who started it know(s) what it even meant—if it meant anything at all.

◆ ◆ ◆

Puzzles by Cicada 3301

First Puzzle (1st Round)
Date - January 4, 2012
Site - 4chan (An anonymous English-language imageboard)

Second Puzzle (2nd Round)
Date - January 5, 2013
Site - 4chan

Third Puzzle (3rd Round)
Date - January 6, 2014
Site - Twitter

Fourth Puzzle (Cicada breaks the silence)
Date - July 27, 2015
Site - Twitter

Fifth Puzzle (New clue)
Date - January 5, 2016
Site - Twitter

ARRIVAL

First Round - 2012

On January 4th, 2012, Cicada 3301 first became known to the public by posting an intriguing message and a photo of a duck on 4Chan.

The message read:

"Hello. We are looking for highly intelligent individuals. To find them, we have devised a test.

There is a message hidden in this image.

Find it, and it will lead you on the road to finding us. We look forward to meeting the few that will make it all the way through.

Good luck.

3301"

It ended with a signature that we all would remember as time went by—3301.

Hello. We are looking for highly intelligent individuals. To find them, we have devised a test.

There is a message hidden in this image.

Find it, and it will lead you on the road to finding us. We look forward to meeting the few that will make it all the way through.

Good luck.

3301

Solving this simply led to more puzzles to complete. As they became increasingly difficult, only a few would move ahead in the race to be recruited or get close to figuring out what Cicada 3301 really is. Soon, other individuals posted in Reddit and chat rooms, anything to communicate and share thoughts on what was really going on here.

Second Round - 2013

It had been exactly 366 days since the 2012 Cicada puzzle began. Nothing had happened in 11 months. Until, on the 5th of January 2013, when a second image was posted on 4chan.
The message read:
"Hello again. Our search for intelligent individuals now continues.
The first clue is hidden within this image.
Find it, and it will lead you on the road to finding us. We look forward to meeting the few that will make it all the way through.
Good luck
3301"

Hello again. Our search for intelligent individuals now continues.

The first clue is hidden within this image.

Find it, and it will lead you on the road to finding us. We look forward to meeting the few that will make it all the way through.

Good luck.

3301

Some have claimed that Cicada 3301 is a secret society with the goal of improving cryptography, privacy, and anonymity. Others have claimed that Cicada 3301 is a cult or religion. According to statements of several people, who claimed to have won the 2012 puzzle, 3301 typically uses non-puzzle-based recruiting methods, but created the Cicada puzzles because they were looking for potential members with cryptography and computer security skills.

Third Round - 2014

Cicada 3301 was back for its third year, and the internet has gone wild. In early January 2014, people gathered together on the net to wait for the next signs of life from Cicada 3301. After several fake puzzles, eventually, a genuine message from Cicada was received. On January 6th, the Twitter account used by Cicada in 2013's puzzle was re-examined; after being inactive for about a year, it suddenly tweeted a link to a picture on Imgur. The message read:
"Hello.
Epiphany is upon us. Your pilgrimage has begun. Enlightment awaits.
Good luck
3301."

Hello.

Epiphany is upon you. Your pilgrimage has begun. Enlightenment awaits.

Good luck.

3301

Twitter comments-

"Dear Holmes, the hunt has begun!"

"Take me to your leader."

"Wish I was a pro on math! This sounds more exciting than Candy Crush!!! "

" Listen 3301. What your doing is illegal. You are forming a secret government. Justice will defeat you. "

" Who the f--- are you m-----f-----"

"Illuminati actually means enlightened and was a real organization. This may have something to do the last sentence."

It's perhaps the most enigmatic and intriguing thing on the internet, which promises an "epiphany" when you solve it. No one knows who set it or what the prize is at the end, but Cicada 3301 has posted mysterious, extremely difficult puzzles for three years in a row, in an attempt to recruit and enlighten the best cryptanalysts from the public.

Fourth Round - 2015

Cicada breaks the silence

No New Puzzle for 2015?
As far as we know, Cicada 3301 has not released a new puzzle for 2015. We were expecting a new puzzle to be released in January 2015, but several months passed and no official word from Cicada 3301. An official message must be signed with Cicada's PGP (Pretty Good Privacy) signature, otherwise the message could be from anyone. A verifiable PGP signature is the only way to prove that a message is genuinely from Cicada 3301, as they are the only people who can use their signature.

At 10:35 P.M. on the 27th of July 2015, Cicada 3301 broke the silence and posted a Pastebin link to their official Twitter account.

The message read:
" -----BEGIN PGP SIGNED MESSAGE-----

Hash: SHA1

Some news organisations have recently claimed that "3301" is tied to the illegal activities of a group that has claimed responsibility for attacks against Planned Parenthood.

We do not engage in illegal activities. We are not associated with this group in any way, nor do condone their use of our name, number, or symbolism.

3301

-----BEGIN PGP SIGNATURE-----
Version: GnuPG v1

iQIcBAEBAgAGBQJVtw9HAAoJEBgfAeV6NQkPIPOP/3JCIXeJw-
MERQ2Ofzduoh3Jo
Ll27XoYWQ5Q2OFL//HCn4fVR3qf5bCh8IlapeW3vq2dLTIPM-
lHf/FPUL9oSWoXN2
3F94PWnGN1GlCvUlNFsUxIxPwR+bP2bzr7dOZry/aW-
rV4RchjYE26xsZp+Vc5w7T
WAT6zX1SA8fhJH4XmJUKsF+7bnIW8TmzUpuHDcYwMGAg-
wQPoxibprFwY+juJp8KV
ZJOW76rU3F18KhHLbDrFUNwDkXddI7mkf8Nsux+I/
Pz0+vqvdFH15nEuv2MORh5w
nYOg3X3duqQ8LLVxmlIIbMIM5hj8I95QnXxebN1b-
p6yn92RvHqKU++1MyQ1f4ivW
KFeNWAtuF47DTcoadBDVRFLrtcYWYFkcRj913i7bT
+Kt3q3pBtdMlP/CAFaO3WwV
fN7jFhTKQIcVGl9RL44CMFCvL1VVUZzT+4SQxLjwSaSfXKN2N-
F9zbPoWGfx9dHHF
fFulsVTQbBMHYaJhGTa6lkPHlJgbtf0kYsRnNnQ1Rk6zSz-
GT6l5fvzMi6ahxro+S
zrPAdjLJK5VXYaI/bVD+qZXTMpa4VbETTUDPgpAKvW6aYz-

uLld4t4v3EbHlDfNyT
XWyqoo3+/JP6VkeSPMyBP4xIdsEiu9jPd0OSmU6UOFPI2O-
H5zAjdoZ/rqMzvO5pk
aZ3Wu1GK9nmbAhMQPNi+
=77uq
-----END PGP SIGNATURE----- "

"No puzzle, only message," the Internet said. It seems that Cicada 3301 wants everyone to refocus their efforts on the unsolved 2014 puzzle.

Fifth Round - 2016

New Clue

After over a year of silence, a mysterious online puzzle has returned with a cryptic tweet. On January 5th, 2016 The anonymous group Cicada 3301 tweeted a link to an image on there twit-

ter handle @1231507051321.
The message read:
"Hello.
The path lies empty; epiphany seeks the devoted.
Liber Primus is the way. Its words are the map, their meaning is the road, and their numbers are the direction.
Seek and you will be found.
Good luck.
3301"

Hello.

The path lies empty; epiphany seeks the devoted.

Liber Primus is the way. Its words are the map, their meaning is the road, and their numbers are the direction.

Seek and you will be found.

Good luck.

3301

Beware false paths. Verify OpenPGP 7A35090F.

The image's message, however, seems only to suggest that solvers go back to something they'd practically given up on: "Liber Primus is the way. Its words are the map, their meaning is the road, and their numbers are the direction."

Liber Primus is the name given to a 76-page book of runes, discovered at the end of the 2014 version of the 3301 puzzle, and it remains largely undeciphered to this day, having been practically abandoned out of frustration.

2016's tweet was the last tweet of the official Cicada 3301 twitter account. A message from Cicada was discovered on Pastebin at the end of April 2017. It read *"Beware false paths. Always verify PGP signature from 7A35090F"*

Raw Paste Data

" -----BEGIN PGP SIGNED MESSAGE-----
Hash: SHA512

Beware false paths. Always verify PGP signature from 7A35090F.

3301

-----BEGIN PGP SIGNATURE-----
Version: CicadaPG v.3301

iQIcBAEBCgAGBQJY5CrwAAoJEBgfAe-
V6NQkPFvMQAJa3W1K1gFcxFPk90fMFFKKx
oEd7wt26sMYE+FIQmaiC/4Eswmys52+joTUft4oSfHuxT79g-
g84EhSPSfyn4IpPD
aJivM4DAbh456bTq3Jk2ZUw97fTBLAHLPQFr/2sY6bmh-
ncTHlx/hRUp2DKXcBccI
Zxl/0SuBiEAfFZuIW3hOS7gnoT409z9f7yKsrw
+WrLjKiqziOle5Ck7u+EBJn75y
XyKEtRmzaMt/OvQGUV2WNErqZgnoq54/WZwTv-
lglIeTrK9t8q5KE80ybWthbdLpK
qtaIgPNN/mvX12Xbnhr6dqN1s7VHOZvjLzFu7j/9RrT90XH-
HTWo9P6GfNTzJkIWC

X+pakY2y+QJXcZhGk3Y7asWX/GGOvbhWnlHIpV-
sESK2JH5e2YFKusjyW2wTzaNQ6
aBSC+3QwxYVVSsETXR8cC4AaCueRmhmOOGC7gDYFLyKroEF-
bX4Ii9TllDV6z67Os
hFE3fhGDcoGdi4Hcs4mFUIgGE1TeD9XpogMSi2uXiZylUEaOKs-
g4spzuiuqI+YLi
8JqcuZ6rQVJ4j1MH95uGuwFzdIIupFLXAZ4NGLz+2Lia
+nmq5e08FjVZ+0zb8cnw
17rLIBMwEgEyu2r5pq4ObToGuWvRIcaFOe7bhBNm9ZYR1
DUVzD+hJ4XQa5jhi23C
s2bdlE5mbHOLUuNuOm50
=6zQ2
-----END PGP SIGNATURE-----"

"No puzzle, only message," the Internet said.

◆ ◆ ◆

THE COMMUNITY

I t has been called "the most elaborate and mysterious puzzle of the internet age" and is listed as one of the "top 5 eeriest, unsolved mysteries of the internet", and much speculation exists as to its function. Many have speculated that the puzzles are a recruitment tool for the NSA, CIA, MI6, a "Masonic conspiracy" or a cyber mercenary group. Others have claimed Cicada 3301 is an alternate reality game. No company or individual has taken credit for it or attempted to monetize it, however.

A growing community of armchair detectives sought to unravel this elaborate puzzle but no one was quite sure what to make of it. Questions like
"What was the puzzle for?"
"Who was behind it?"
"What happens when you reach the end?"
were all over the internet since 2012. Some naturally dismissed it as an elaborate joke while others perceived its complexity as evidence against it being the work of a mere troll.
Before long rumors began to circulate that this could be the work of some secret society or intelligence agency with the intent of recruiting individuals proficient in cryptography, steganography and other related fields. Whoever is behind this intricate game had the foresight to include an authentication code known as PGP signature along with every clue, to verify that an image or message is actually from Cicada 3301.

Liber Primus is a book written by Cicada 3301. Discovered in 2013, this book is primarily written in runes.

Translation

Most things are not worth preserving.

Adherence:

We follow dogma so that we can belong and be right or we follow reason so we can belong and be right.

There is nothing to be right about; to belong is death.

It is the behavio'rs of consumption, preservation, and adher-en[ce].

The Leaked Email of The Community

At the end of the first puzzle, finalists supposedly received this email

Actual Email

DO NOT SHARE THIS INFORMATION!

Congratulations your month of testing has come to an end out of the thousands who attempted it you are one of only a few who have succeeded.

There is one last step although there will not be any hidden codes or secret messages or physical treasure hunts this last step is only honesty we have always been honest with you and we shall continue to be honest with you and we expect you to be honest with us in return.

You have all wondered who we are and so we shall now tell you we are an international group we have no name we have no symbol we have no membership rosters we do not have a public website and we do not advertise ourselves we are a group of individuals who have proven
ourselves much like you have by completing this recruitment contest and we are drawn together by common beliefs a careful reading of the texts used in the contest would have revealed some of these beliefs that tyranny and oppression of any kind must end that censorship is wrong and that privacy is an inalienable right.

We are not a *hacker* group nor are we a *warez* group we do not engagein illegal activity nor do our members if you are engaged in illegal activity we ask that you cease any and all illegal activities or decline membership at this time we will not ask questions if you decline however if you lie to us we will find out.

You are undoubtedly wondering what it is that we do we are much like a *think tank* in that our primary focus is on researching and developing techniques to aid the ideas we advocate liberty privacy security you have undoubtedly heard of a few of our past projects and if you choose to accept membership we are happy to have you on-board to help with future projects.

Please reply to this email with the answers to the next few questions to continue:

* Do you believe that every human being has a right to privacy and anonymity and is within their rights to use tools which help obtain and maintain privacy cash strong encryption anonymity software etc?

* Do you believe that information should be free?

* Do you believe that censorship harms humanity?

We look forward to hearing from you.

3301

There also have been allegations of Cicada of being a hacker group. They were accused of being part of illegal activities as a hacker group calling themselves "3301." A hacker group of the same name hacked Planned Parenthood, a global NPO providing reproductive care. But later, the hacker team confirmed that they are in no way associated with the puzzle group Cicada 3301. Even Cicada commented to this with a PGP-signed message and denied any involvement in any illegal activities.

Amidst all the speculations and accusations, the search is still on for the faces behind the Cicada 3301 puzzles.

Since 2012 many sites are making assumptions about Cicada 3301 Community. At some point forums on Dark Web were filled by Cicada 3301 topic.

Dark Web on Cicada 3301

People speculate that:
- Cicadia 3301 is an actual group, started and run by legit members.
- People have completed the final puzzle, which allowed them to message Cicadia 3301 themselves
- Cicadia 3301 is a culmination of powerful world figures unknown by the common folk
- Once you join, the world will never know of or hear from you again

It has also been told that 1 man was able to join and then leave Cicadia 3301 successfully. He is claimed to have left a text dump somewhere on the dark web. I have read the supposed "Cicadia 3301" member dump and, though I cannot find the old link, in it I remember him claiming:

- He was met by military personal after meeting at the arranged contact location
- He was asked to play chess with a man he had never heard of before, yet claimed to be very powerful
- He was asked various questions about Biology, Computer Science, and the Arts
- He claimed he became part of a world wide think tank
- He claimed to have escaped under guise of a deceased member, wherein he anonymously wrote a variety of documents on Cicadia 3301 and then left the text dump of them on the DW.

"With Cicada, no one knows what the goal is," says one cipher expert, "or how you know when you won."

◆ ◆ ◆

THE THEORIES

Cicadian

"A Cicadian is someone who has chosen to give up the superficial and unfulfilling world around them to follow the path of the Cicada, and emerge into enlightenment."
- 3301

Cicadianism

"Cicadianism is a technomystical order. Our philosophy is neither a religion nor a science, but a blend of spirituality, technology, science, and mysticism. We refer to it as a 'technomysticism'."

Cicada 3301 is the other side. Think about this.. you live in a world ran by your government. Your government runs your media, runs your education, and runs your religions. You only truly 'know' what your government tells you. There is, however, another side. Some people live freely within this world and they fight a battle much bigger than one can see. The government is at war, and it's not a terrorist with a bomb strapped to his chest. Cicada 3301 puzzles are meant to find and attract other 'special' individuals. These individuals possess something quite special and amazing.

A self-claimed Cicada 3301
member statement

" Cicada 3301 has often been referred to as "the most elaborate and mysterious puzzle of the internet age" and has been listed as one of the "top 5 eeriest, unsolved mysteries of the internet". Many have speculated that behind Cicada is NSA, CIA etc and yet others speculate that Cicada is an alternative reality game among many other theories. You have all wondered who we are, and so we shall now tell you. We are an international group. We have no membership rosters. We do not have a public website and we do not advertise ourselves. We are a group of individuals who have proven ourselves, much like you have, by completing this recruitment contest, and we are drawn together by common beliefs.

A careful reading of the texts used in the contest would have revealed some of these beliefs: that knowledge must be free, that censorship is wrong and all those who built their reputation based on imaginary beliefs that they create for selfish profit must end. And it will.

Cicada is a technomystical order. Our philosophy is neither a religion nor a science, but a blend of spirituality, technology, science, and mysticism. We are more closely related to Demonolatry, which after the numerious texts,scripts and unpublished cryptic books (including the notorious Liber Primus) we have decoded after all these many years, we like to call our path

Demonurgy. And so it begins....
We started the Cicada project back on 2012, when a member of our order provided us with some very old, encoded family grimories. It is pointless to waste time analyzing the riddles of 2012, 2013 and 2014, because those who solve them release everything on the internet. For this reason, Cicada shut them out.
We were seeking individuals who have with expert skills in a varying range of disciplines including steganography, cryptography, Gematria and ancient Mayan numerology, as well as detailed understandings of 18th century European literature. And we found them. It was at this point Cicada shuts its doors and started working. In our order there exist no application requirements for membership, like as we see with other orders or Temples. WE choose our members. We are in almost every group and forum, even as members of other orders. We like to be involved but most of all we like to observe - even the observers! We don't keep records of our members, most of them are in our order with aliases. We don't run backgrounds checks or demand full transparency because we know who the persons are that we choose to become members of Cicada.

All those years that we were working and at the same time observed, we grew sick and tired of the "famous" occultists. Did you make enough money based on imaginary theories? Did you build a strong reputation based on marketing? We see these people as members of several groups, but never reply to nor help the new people on this path. If you seek help, you must buy their books! Or their online courses! This must stop. And it will! Demonic will, and does provide all the information that you need for free, who are you that you dare sell them for personal profit? Decoding the Liber Primus gave us knowledge that even we couldn't believe. We obtained the knowledge to work straight with the Divine, even spiritual, but most importantly by using devices. All the cultures from Ancient Greece, Egypt, Sumerians, Maya, etc, worked with the devices. Even Atlantis had a very complex mechanism, very similar to our radars. Ofcourse we will start to release all of them in the upcoming months publicly, for free.

By far, the most popular Hierarchies with which the majority of you are working, are the Goetic and the Dukante's hierarchies. The truth that must be told is, that the Demons from both Hierarchies are exist. For example, you will find rituals to Agathodaemon in the ancient Greeks texts and religion where they honor him as the Demon of vineyards and grain fields. So, Richard Dukante didn't discover something new, leaving his workings rooms for serious doubts. Dukante' himself was unfortunately seen as lunatic by most of the occult community. Dukante' wrote some 25 books on demonolatry (known as the Dukante' Grimores) but they remain as yet unpublished in the hands of his daughter, Selinda Dukante. No one has ever seen those grimores. Do they exist? If so what information do they contain? Are they writings about the Demonic or is just random babblings of a man whom the occult community accuses as a lunatic?

We didn't one day just up and decide to appear or create our order that we kept secret for so many years, just for fun. We appear to effect change. To share what we have found all those years with the rest of our community. We

do not support Traditional Demonolatry as it stands today, secretive and exclusive. There is a marked sense of if you're not a traditional Demonolator then you're not worthy of learning the mysteries. This must ends. And it will. Who decides the definition of the "Tradition"? Ten Demonolatry families about whom no one knows, with whom no one is familiar. And even if we know some of them, who gave them the right to decide and define the path and the connection with the Demonic? We neither support nor tolerate methods of oligarchy.

In the upcoming months, you will have the opportunity to see with your own eyes, the lies that they have been feeding you all these years and how they used the Demonic to create highly profitable businesses for personal gain. These, the "Dedicated Demonolators".

We already know that our statements will stir the pot and create debates. Some of you may agree, others disagree. That is called Democracy and Free Speech. Here in our order, the usual methods that the famous occultists use, like making an author disappear because that author's work threatens that of the "famous occultists" does not work here. It is time to step back from the occult, if you see and on your own that your books don't sell anymore. Maybe it is time to start deal with the things that make you happy! The multiple partners, your BDSM forums, the weird magical practices in your basements, etc!

Allow the beginners to take the knowledge for which they are searching and deserve, and move forward to find the divinity within and emerge. That's all for now. In the upcoming weeks we will open Cicada to the public. We will share the rituals, the spells and all that we have gained all these years with all of you. "Truth cannot be seen, cannot be thought, cannot be sensed, cannot be heard, cannot be smelled... Truth can be, has to be, Truth is...."
http://1711141131131.xyz/
Cicada is not involved in illegal activities or hacking in any way, shape or form. "

A Brain Network?

They have answers and secrets hidden in their Liber Primus for any who would find them. They are waiting to unlock you from yourself and your reality.

'PROGRAM YOUR MIND
PROGRAM REALITY'

Cicada is the coming tide of evolutionary change. The idea is designed to spread memetically resulting in subtle shifts in the host organism's consciousness. Ultimately these changes will result in the connection of every consciousness to every other consciousness, resulting in a global brain/consciousness.

Cicada is the brain network.

3301 is global consciousness using us to create himself.

Cicada 3301 is a fucking A.I..
And its creators lost control of it..

THE BOOK

At the beginning of 2014, it was time for round three. This time, the puzzle seemed to revolve around a strange book. The 76 pages book was titled *Liber Primus* meaning 'First Book' in Latin and evidently written by Cicada.

The runic alphabet uncovered in 2013 finally made sense as the book was primarily written in runes. The meaning of translated pages were cryptic at best. The book consisted of various philosophical and ideological ideas and appear to be their manifesto.

Many have since compared the strange writings to that of a cult. The book also contains a bunch of clues and codes.

Cover

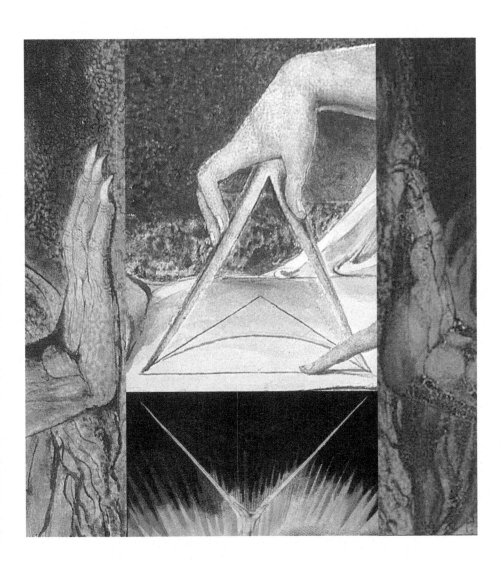

Liber Primus

Liber Primus

A Warning

Translation

A WARNING

BELIEVE NOTHING FROM THIS BOOK
EXCEPT WHAT YOU KNOW TO BE TRUE
TEST THE KNOWLEDGE
FIND YOUR TRUTH
EXPERIENCE YOUR DEATH
DO NOT EDIT OR CHANGE THIS BOOK
OR THE MESSAGE CONTAINED WITHIN
EITHER THE WORDS OR THEIR NUMBERS
FOR ALL IS SACRED

Chapter 1

Intus

Welcome

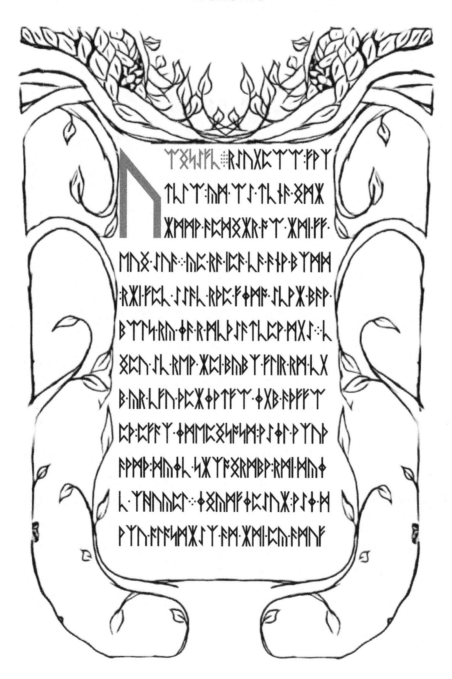

Translation

WELCOME
WELCOME, PILGRIM, TO THE GREAT JOURNEY TO-
WARD THE END OF ALL THINGS

IT IS NOT AN EASY TRIP, BUT FOR THOSE WHO FIND
THEIR WAY HERE IT IS A NECESSARY ONE

ALONG THE WAY YOU WILL FIND AN END TO ALL
STRUGGLE AND SUFFERING, YOUR INNOCENCE, YOUR
ILLUSIONS, YOUR CERTAINTY, AND YOUR REALITY

ULTIMATELY, YOU WILL DISCOVER AN END TO SELF

Translation

_IT IS THROUGH THIS PILGRIMAGE THAT WE SHAPE OURSELVES
AND OUR REALITIES
JOURNEY DEEP WITHIN AND YOU WILL ARRIVE OUTSIDE_

_LIKE THE INSTAR, IT IS ONLY THROUGH GOING WITHIN THAT WE
MAY EMERGE_

WISDOM

YOU ARE A BEING UNTO YOURSELF

YOU ARE A LAW UNTO YOURSELF

EACH INTELLIGENCE IS HOLY

FOR ALL THAT LIVES IS HOLY

AN INSTRUCTION COMMAND YOUR OWN SELF

ᛋᛈᛖᛗ ᛈᛁᛋᛉᛖᛗ᛬ᚦᛖ ᚲᚱᛁᛉᛗᛋ ᚠᚱᛖ ᛋᚠᛚ

ᚱᛗᛉ᛬᛬ᚦᛖ ᛏᚠᛏᛁᛗᛁᛏ ᚠᛟᛚ ᛏᚷᛁ᛬ᛁᛋᚠ

ᛚᚱᛗᛉ᛬᛬ᚠᛚᛚ ᚦᛟᛋ ᛋᛁᚠᛚᛏᛉ ᛒᛖ ᛗᛁᛋᚱᛗ

ᚲᛏᛗᛉ᛬᛬

ᛚ ᛏᚠᚠ ᛈᛁ᛬᛬

272	138	ᛁᛋᚱᛉᛉᚠᛋ	131	151
ᚠᛈᛗᚱᛏᛏ	ᛒᛟᚠᚠᛗᚱᛋ	ᛉᛁᛉ	ᛚᛈᚱᛁᛏ	18
226	ᚠᛒᛋᛚᛉᚱ	ᚠᚠᚱᛖ	245	ᛗᚠᛒᛁᛁᛋ
18	ᚠᛁᛏᛏᚠᚷ	ᛉᛁᛉ	ᛗᛖᛋᚱᛁᛋᛋ	ᚠᛈᛗᚱᛏᛏ
151	131	ᛚᛉᛒᛏ	138	272

Translation

SOME WISDOM
THE PRIMES ARE SACRED
THE TOTIENT FUNCTION IS SACRED
ALL THINGS SHOULD BE ENCRYPTED
KNOW THIS

272	138	shadows	131	151
aethereal	*buffers*	*void*	*carnal*	*18*
226	*obscura*	*form*	*245*	*mobius*
18	*analog*	*void*	*mournful*	*aethereal*
151	*131*	*cabal*	*138*	*272*

272 138 341 131 151

366 199 130 320 18

226 245 91 245 226

18 320 130 199 366

151 131 341 138 272

Translation

A KOAN
A MAN DECIDED TO GO AND STUDY WITH A MASTER

HE WENT TO THE DOOR OF THE MASTER

"WHO ARE YOU WHO WISHES TO STUDY HERE" ASKED THE MASTER

THE STUDENT TOLD THE MASTER HIS NAME

"THAT IS NOT WHO YOU ARE, THAT IS ONLY WHAT YOU ARE CALLED

WHO ARE YOU WHO WISHES TO STUDY HERE" HE ASKE

Translation

D AGAIN

THE MAN THOUGHT FOR A MOMENT, AND REPLIED "I AM A PROFESSOR"

"THAT IS WHAT YOU DO, NOT WHO YOU ARE," REPLIED THE MASTER

"WHO ARE YOU WHO WISHES TO STUDY HERE"

CONFUSED, THE MAN THOUGHT SOME MORE

FINALLY, HE ANSWERED, "I AM A HUMAN BEING"

"THAT IS ONLY YOUR SPECIES, NOT WHO YOU ARE

WE

Translation

O ARE YOU WHO WISHES TO STUDY HERE", ASKED THE MASTER AGAIN
AFTER A MOMENT OF THOUGHT, THE PROFESSOR REPLIED "I AM A CONSCIOUSNESS INHABITING AN ARBITRARY BODY"

"THAT IS MERELY WHAT YOU ARE, NOT WHO YOU ARE

WHO ARE YOU WHO WISHES TO STUDY HERE"

THE MAN WAS GETTING IRRITATED

"I AM," HE STARTED,

Translation

BUT HE COULD NOT THINK OF ANYTHING ELSE TO SAY, SO HE TRAILED OFF
AFTER A LONG PAUSE THE MASTER REPLIED, "THEN YOU ARE WELCOME TO COME STUDY"

AN INSTRUCTION

DO FOUR UNREASONABLE THINGS EACH DAY

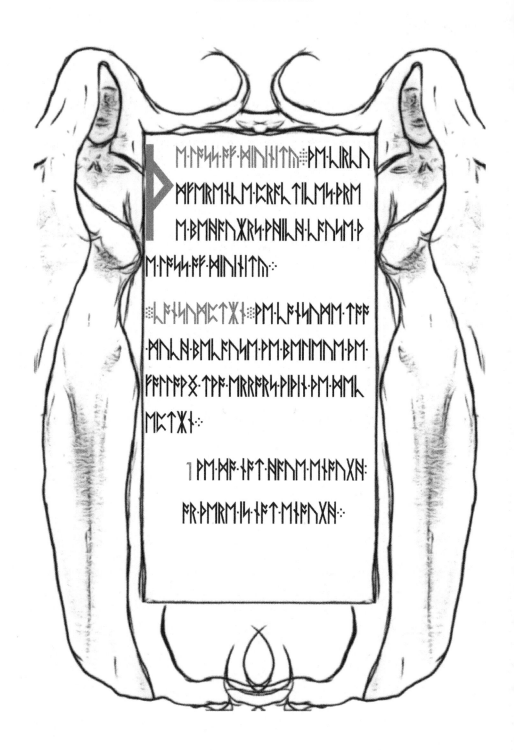

Translation

THE LOSS OF DIVINITY
THE CIRCUMFERENCE PRACTICES THREE BEHAVIORS WHICH CAUSE THE LOSS OF DIVINITY

CONSUMPTION

WE CONSUME TOO MUCH BECAUSE WE BELEIVE THE FOLLWING TWO ERRORS WITHIN THE DECEPTION

1. WE DO NOT HAVE ENOUGH, OR THERE IS NOT ENOUGH

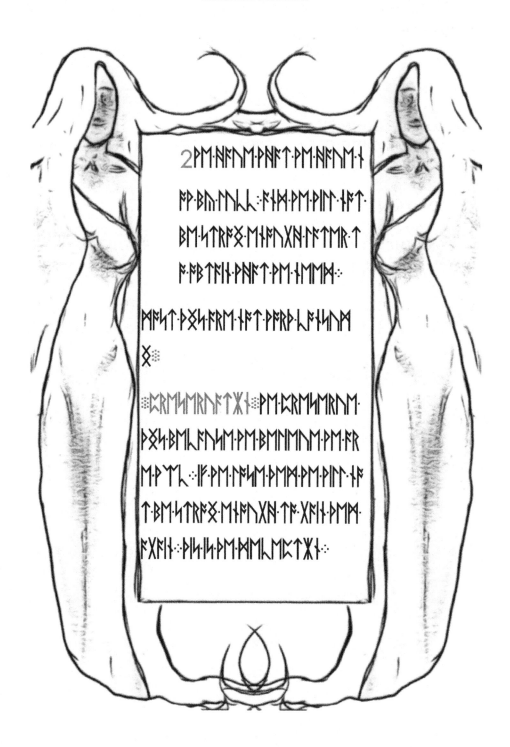

Translation

2. WE HAVE WHAT WE HAVE NOW BY LUCK; AND WE WILL NOT BE STRONG ENOUGH LATER TO OBTAIN WHAT WE NEED MOST THINGS ARE NOT WORTH CONSUMING

PRESERVATION

WE PRESERVE THINGS BECAUSE WE BELIEVE WE ARE WEAK

IF WE LOSE THEM WE WILL NOT BE STRONG ENOUGH TO GAIN THEM AGAIN

THIS IS THE DECEPTION

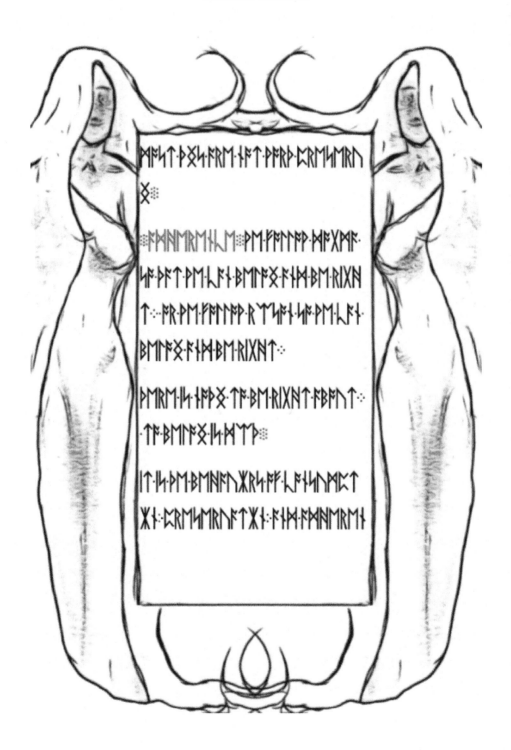

Translation

MOST THINGS ARE NOT WORTH PRESERVING
ADHERENCE

WE FOLLOW DOGMA SO THAT WE CAN BELONG AND BE RIGHT;
OR WE FOLLOW REASON SO WE CAN BELONG AND BE RIGHT

THERE IS NOTHING TO BE RIGHT ABOUT; TO BELONG IS DEATH

IT IS THE BEHAVIORS OF CONSUMPTION, PRESERVATION, AND
ADHEREN

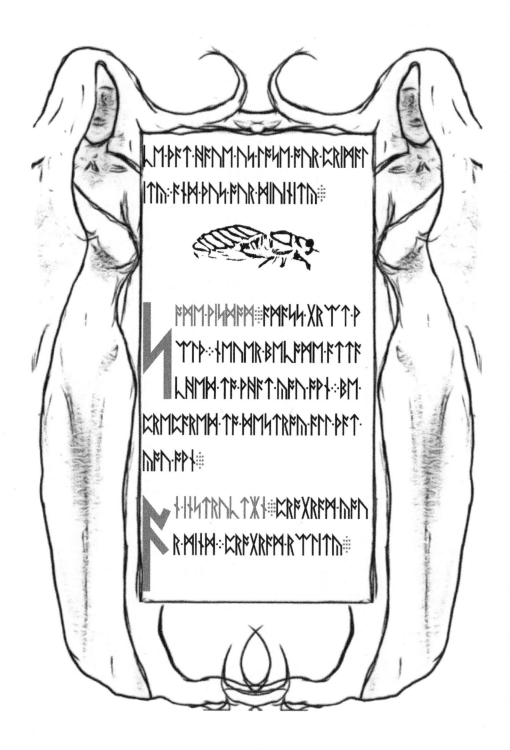

Translation

CE THAT HAVE US LOSE OUR PRIMALITY, AND THUS OUR DIVINITY

SOME WISDOM

AMASS GREAT WEALTH

NEVER BECOME ATTACHED TO WHAT YOU OWN

BE PREPARED TO DESTROY ALL THAT YOU OWN

AN INSTRUCTION

PROGRAM YOUR MIND

PROGRAM REALITY

ᚨ·ᛋᚹᚨᛁ⁝ᛈᚢᛟᚨ·ᛈ·ᚠᛗᚱᛋᛈᛈ:ᚹᛞ·ᚾᚨᚱ
ᛚᚹᛈ·ᛗᚨᛈᚢ ᛉᛁᚾᛞ·ᛚᛟ·ᛉ⁘"ᛰᛗ·
ᛉ·ᛁᚨ·ᚷᛗ·ᚦᛟᛁᛞᛟ·ᛟᚠ·ᛰᛗ·ᛞᛁᛉᚾᚢ
ᛚᚠᚨᚱᚹᛈᛞᚷ:"ᚨᚹ·ᛋᛚ ᛉᛞ⁘ᚨᚷᛗᚷ·ᛉᚱ
ᛉᛗᛇ·ᛒᚹ·ᛉ·ᛋᛒᛚᛞᚹᛈᛚ·ᚠᚠ·ᚹ ᛉᛞᚠᚠᛰᛉ
·ᚹᛖ ᛉᛚ·ᛰᚠᛚ·ᛞᚾᛈᛏ⁚ᚠᚨ·ᛞᛈᛞᛚᚷᚱ·ᚱᚠ
ᛚᚷ"ᛒ·ᚠᛋ·ᛈ·ᛚᛟᛞᛚᚹ·ᛞᛞᚠᚨ·ᛖᛟᛚᛟ·ᛒ
ᛉᛇ"⁘"ᛁᚱᚹᚾ'ᛒ·ᚷᚠᛞᛟ·ᛈ·ᚨᛉᛚ ᛉ·ᛉ
ᚾ·ᛚᛏ·ᚨᛒᚷ:"·ᛚᛇᚢᚠᚨᛖ·ᚷᛗ·ᛏᚷᚢᛇᛟᚷᚠ:
ᚠᚷᛞ·ᛗᛟ·ᚱᚠᚠᛋᚹᚷ·ᛖᛞᛋ·ᛖᚠᛞᚷ·ᛏᚱ·ᚷᛗ
ᚾᚠ·ᛚᚷ·ᛞᛈᛋᛖᛟᚱ⁘ᚠᚨ·ᛞᛈᛞᛚᚷᚱ·ᚱᛏᛈᛒ

Translation

A KOAN

DURING A LESSON, THE MASTER EXPLAINED THE I

"THE I IS THE VOICE OF THE CIRCUMFERENCE," HE SAID

WHEN ASKED BY A STUDENT TO EXPLAIN WHAT THAT MEANT; THE MASTER SAID "IT IS A VOICE INSIDE YOUR HEAD"

"I DON'T HAVE A VOICE IN MY HEAD," THOUGHT THE STUDENT, AND HE RAISED HIS HAND TO TELL THE MASTER

THE MASTER STOP

ᚳᛈᛣ·ᚹᚹ·ᛗᚢᛁᚼᛈᛏᚾ·ᛏᛁᚠ·ᛚᛏᚷ''ᛏᚷ·
ᚾᚼᛁᚱ·ᚹᚠᚷ·ᚦᛗᛗᛚ·ᚠᚠᛏᚼᚹᚹᚾ·ᛏᚤᚾ
ᚹᚳᚷᛁᚠᛏᛚ·ᛏ·ᛏᛏ·ᚷᚼᚾᚼ·ᛁᛒᚠ··ᛁᚱᚦᛏ·
ᛏ··''ᚠᛁᚳ·ᚹᚹ·ᛗᚢᛁᚼᛈᛏᚾᚼᚹᛗᛗᛗ·ᚹᚳᛏ
ᛗᚷᚼᛏᛏᚷᛗᚠ⸬

66

Translation

PED THE STUDENT, AND SAID "THE VOICE THAT JUST SAID YOU HAVE NO VOICE IN YOUR HEAD; IS THE I"

AND THE STUDENTS WERE ENLIGHTENED

ᚠᚻᛁᛋᛏᚱᚾᚷ ᛏᛉᚷᛁ ᚼᚹᛗᛋᛏᛉᛁ ᚠᚱᚲ
ᚦᛉᛋ ᚻᛁᛋᚹ ᚠᚾᛗᚱ ᛏᚱᚾᚹ ᛁᛏᛋᛁᛁᚼᛗ
ᛗᚠᚾᚱᛋᛗᛏᚼ ᚠᚱᚲᚠᛒ ᛗᚼᚾᚱ ᛏᚱᚾ
ᚦ ᛁᚾᚲᚠᛁᛗ ᛁᚠᛉᛉ ᚠᛁ ᚠᛝᛗᚱᛋ

ᛁ ᛁᛏᛒ ᚦᛁᛋ

434	1311	312	278	966
204	812	934	280	1071
626	620	809	620	626
1071	280	934	812	204
966	278	312	1311	434

Translation

AN INSTRUCTION

*KWESTION ALL THINGS DISCOVER TRUTH INSIDE YOURSELF FOL-
LOW YOUR TRUTH IMPOSE NOTHING ON OTHERS*

KNOW THIS

434 1311 312 278 966
204 812 934 280 1071
626 620 809 620 626
1071 280 934 812 204
966 278 312 1311 434

56 Unsolved Pages

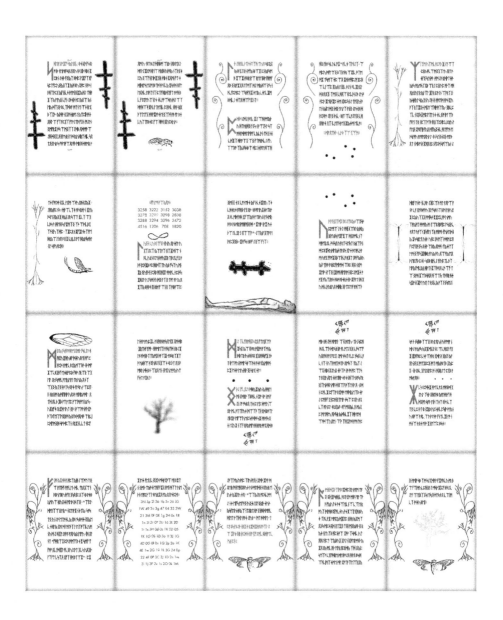

An End

36367763ab73783c7af284446c
59466b4cd653239a311cb7116
d4618dee09a8425893dc7500b
464fdaf1672d7bef5e891c6e227
4568926a49fb4f45132c2a8b4

Translation

AN END

WITHIN THE DEEP WEB, THERE EXISTS A PAGE THAT HASHES TO

36367763ab73783c7af284446c

59466b4cd653239a311cb7116

d4618dee09a8425893dc7500b

464fdaf1672d7bef5e891c6e227

4568926a49fb4f45132c2a8b4
IT IS THE DUTY OF EVERY PILGRIM TO SEEK OUT THIS PAGE

(The community advised participants to seek out a website on the deep web/dark web but the site remains undiscovered)

Parable

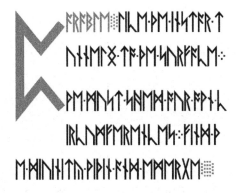

Translation

Parable :

Like the instar tunneling to the surface.

We must shed our own circumferences.

Find the divinity within and emerge.

It's a manifesto for those of us who aren't capable of reaching a deeper fellowship. The Eleusinian Mystery schools had a similar method of giving one story to the normies and something far greater to those who could perceive their hidden signs. It would be nice if some of the losers came back and finished deciphering the book, but maybe they don't want to risk being disqualified from the next round.

◆ ◆ ◆

CRACKING THE
CODE - 2012

It all started on January 4th, 2012. 4chan's users were greeted with a mysterious image.

Hello. We are looking for highly intelligent individuals. To find them, we have devised a test.

There is a message hidden in this image.

Find it, and it will lead you on the road to finding us. We look forward to meeting the few that will make it all the way through.

Good luck.

3301

Opening the main image file using a text editor a cipher string of semi-readable text could be found at the end.

'Tiberius Cladius Caesar says
"lxxt> 33m2mqkyv2gsq3q = w]O2ntk"'

Deciphered to a URL
"http://i.imgur.com/m9sYK.jpg"

The URL leads to this image.

The words "out" and "guess" in the image leads to a text editor name OutGuess. Running the duck image through OutGuess revealed yet another text file.

Here is a book code. To find the book, and more information, go to **http://www.reddit.com/r/a2e7j6ic78hOj/**

1:20, 2:3, 3:5, 4:20, 5:5, 6:53, 7:1, 8:8, 9:2, 10:4, 11:8, 12:4, 13:13, 14:4, 15:8, 16:4, 17:5, 18:14, 19:7, 20:31, 21:12, 22:36, 23:2, 24:3, 25:5, 26:65, 27:5, 28:1, 29:2, 30:18, 31:32, 32:10, 33:3, 34:25, 35:10, 36:7, 37:20, 38:10, 39:32, 40:4, 41:40, 42:11, 43:9, 44:13, 45:6, 46:3, 47:5, 48:43, 49:17, 50:13, 51:4, 52:2, 53:18, 54:4, 55:6, 56:4, 57:24, 58:64, 59:5, 60:37, 61:60, 62:12, 63:6, 64:8, 65:5, 66:18, 67:45, 68:10, 69:2, 70:17, 71:9, 72:20, 73:2, 74:34, 75:13, 76:21

Good luck.

3301

The link in the text file leads to a subreddit. The subreddit contains lots of different text posts and two images labeled "Welcome" and "Problems?".

Welcome

Problems?

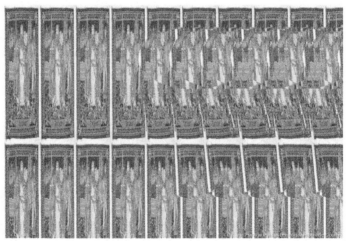

When opening these images in OutGuess each image contains a message.

Welcome's message

-----BEGIN PGP SIGNED MESSAGE-----
Hash: SHA1

- From here on out, we will cryptographically sign all messages with this key.

It is available on the mit keyservers. Key ID 7A35090F, as posted in a2e7j6ic78h0j.

Patience is a virtue.

Good luck.

3301
-----BEGIN PGP SIGNATURE-----
Version: GnuPG v1.4.11 (GNU/Linux)

iQIcBAEBAgAGBQJPBRz7AAoJEBgfAeV6NQkP1UIQALFcO8DyZ-
kecTK5pAIcGez7k
ewjGBoCfjfO2NlRROuQm5CteXiH3Te5G+5ebsdRmGWVca-
h8QzN4UjxpKcTQRPB9e
/ehVI5BiBJq8GlOnaSRZpzsYobwK-
H6Jy6haAr3kPFK1lOXXyHSiNnQbydGw9BFRI
fSr//DY86BUILE8sGJR6FA8Vzjiifcv6mmXkk3ICrT8z0qY7m/
wFOYjgiSohvYpg
x5biG6TBwxfmXQOaITdO5rO8+4mtLnP//qN7E9zjTYj4Z4g-
Bhdf6hPSuOqjh1s+6
/C6IehRChpx8gwpdhIlNf1coz/Zigg-
Piqdj75Tyqg88lEr66fVVB2d7PGObSyYSp
HJl8llrt8Gnk1UaZUS6/eCjnBniV/BLfZPVD2VFKH2Vvvty8sL
+S8hCxsuLCjydh
skpshcjMVV9xPIEYzwSEaqBqOZMdNFEPxJzC0XISlWSfx-
ROm85r3NYvbrx9lwVbP
mUpLKFn8ZcMbf7UX18frgOtujmqqUvDQ2dQhmCUywPdtsK-
HFLc1xIqdrnRWUS3CD
eejUzGYDB5lSflujTjLPgGvtlCBW5ap00cfIHUZPOzmJWoEzgFgd-
Nc9iIkcUUlke
e2WbYwCCuwSlLsdQRMA//PJN+a1h2ZMSzzMbZsr/YXQDU-
WvEaYI8MckmXEkZmDoA

RL0xkbHEFVGBmoMPVzeC
=fRcg
-----END PGP SIGNATURE-----

Problem's Message

-----BEGIN PGP SIGNED MESSAGE-----
Hash: SHA1

The key has always been right in front of your eyes.

This isn't the quest for the Holy Grail. Stop making it more difficult than it is.

Good luck.

3301
-----BEGIN PGP SIGNATURE-----

Version: GnuPG v1.4.11 (GNU/Linux)

iQIcBAEBAgAGBQJPCBl3AAoJEBgfAeV6NQkPo6EQAKghp7Z-
KYxmsYM96iNQu5GZV
fbjUHsEL164ZLctGkgZx2H1HyYFEc6FGvcfzqs43vV/IzN4m-
K0SMy2qFPfjuG2JJ
tv3x2QfHMM3M2+dwX30bUD12UorMZNrLo8HjT-
panYD9hL8WglbSIBJhnLE5CPlUS
BZRSx0yh1U+wbnlTQBxQIOxLkPIz+xCMBwSKl5BaCb006z43/
HJt7NwynqWXJmVV
KScmkpFC3ISEBcYKhHHWv1IPQnFqMdW4dExXdRqWuwC-
shXpGXwDoOXfKVp5NW7Ix
9kCyfC7XC4iWXymGgd+/h4ccFFVm+WWOczOq/zeME
+0vJhJqvj+fN2MZtvckpZbc
CMfLjn1z4w4d7mkbEpVjgVIU8/+KClNFPSf4asqjBKdrcCE-
MAl80vZorElG6OVIH
aLV4XwqiSu0LEF1ESCqbxkEmqp7U7CHl2VW6qv0h0Gxy+/
UT0W1NoLJTzLBFiOzy
QIqqpgVg0dAFs74SlIf3oUTxt6IUpQX5+uo8kszMHTJQRP7K22/
A3cc/VS/2Ydg4
o6OfN54Wcq+8IMZxEx+vxtmRJCUROVpHTTQ5unmy-
G9zQATxn8byD9Us070FAg6/v
jGjo1VVUxn6HX9HKxdx4wYGMP5grmD8k4jQdF1Z7GtbcqzD-
sxP65XCaOYmray1Jy
FG5OlgFyOflmjBXHsNad
=SqLP
-----END PGP SIGNATURE-----

Both of them were signed with PGP signatures, which are basically a completely secure method of ensuring that the message has come from the confirmed sender.

In the header of the subreddit there is a number sequence that is written using Mayan numbers as follows:

10 2 14 7 19 6 18 12 7 8 17 0 19

Mayan Numbers

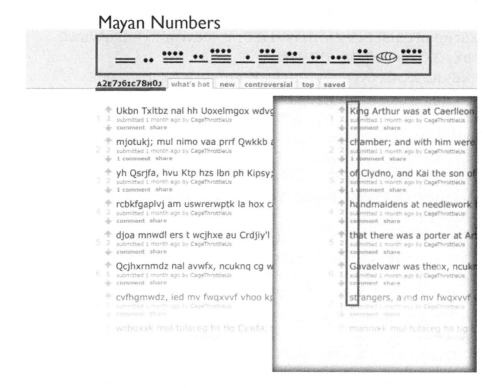

Comparing this with the **a2e7j6ic78h0j7eiejd0120** in the title, we can see that numbers below 10 in the sequence above is also found in this string, at the same positions. Also note that instead of 10 we have "a", instead of 14 we have "e", and so on up to "j" being 19.

Since the title of the page contains 23 characters and there were only 13 mayan numbers is quite likely that we are supposed to continue converting characters from the title to numbers

Later was found that key was derived from King Arthur's text (Image).
Translate each digit to a letter (from alphabet starting with A = 0) and you get **kcohtgsmhirathosotnabca**... Each letter is the first letter in lines of decrypted text (Image)
Each letter in each string is meant to be shifted by the number corresponding to it's location in the text. This leads to yet another book.

The Mabinogion

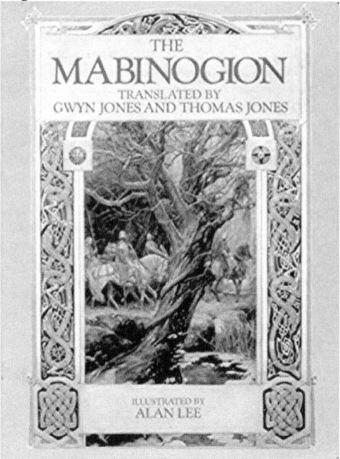

The Mabinogion, by Translated by Lady Charlotte Guest

THE LADY OF THE FOUNTAIN

King Arthur was at Caerlleon upon Usk; and one day he sat in his chamber; and with him were Owain the son of Urien, and Kynon the son of Clydno, and Kai the son of Kyner; and Gwenhwyvar and her handmaidens at needlework by the window. And if it should be said that there was a porter at Arthur's palace, there was none. Glewlwyd Gavaelvawr was there, acting as porter, to welcome guests and strangers, and to receive them with honour, and to inform them of the manners and customs of the Court; and to direct those who came to the Hall or to the presence-chamber, and those who came to take up their lodging.

In the centre of the chamber King Arthur sat upon a seat of green rushes, over which was spread a covering of flame-coloured satin, and a cushion of red satin was under his elbow.

Then Arthur spoke, "If I thought you would not disparage me," said he, "I would sleep while I wait for my repast; and you can entertain one another with relating tales, and can obtain a flagon of mead and some meat from Kai." And the King went to sleep. And Kynon the son of Clydno asked Kai for that which Arthur had promised them. "I, too, will have the good tale which he promised to me," said Kai. "Nay," answered Kynon, "fairer will it be for thee to fulfill Arthur's behest, in the first place, and then we will tell thee the best tale that we know." So Kai went to the

kcohtgsmhirathosotnabca...

This is the code we found from the duck image's text file.

Key 1

1:20, 2:3, 3:5, 4:20, 5:5, 6:53, 7:1, 8:8, 9:2, 10:4, 11:8, 12:4, 13:13, 14:4, 15:8, 16:4, 17:5, 18:14, 19:7, 20:31, 21:12, 22:36, 23:2, 24:3, 25:5, 26:65, 27:5, 28:1, 29:2, 30:18, 31:32, 32:10, 33:3, 34:25, 35:10, 36:7, 37:20, 38:10, 39:32, 40:4, 41:40, 42:11, 43:9, 44:13, 45:6, 46:3, 47:5, 48:43, 49:17, 50:13, 51:4, 52:2, 53:18, 54:4, 55:6, 56:4, 57:24, 58:64, 59:5, 60:37, 61:60, 62:12, 63:6, 64:8, 65:5, 66:18, 67:45, 68:10, 69:2, 70:17, 71:9, 72:20, 73:2, 74:34, 75:13, 76:21

From the book we found

Key 2
kcohtgsmhirathosotnabca...

There are 76 codes in key 1. Each code contains 2 numbers. The first number is the line, which is "K" in Key 2, and the second number is the character in that line, Starting from K (King) to 20th letter which is **C** (Caerlleon). So from the first code of key 1 we found **C**. Continuing this till the last code will lead to a message.

Call us at us telephone numBer two one four three nine oh nine six oh eight.

2143909608

A telephone number. This number has since deactivated. Calling this number initially gave the following message:

Very good. You have done well. There are three prime numbers associated with the original final.jpg image. 3301 is one of them. You will have to find the other two. Multiply all three of these numbers together and add a .com to find the next step. Good luck. Goodbye.

The original image had the dimensions of **509** and **503**, both of which are prime numbers. These, when multiplied with **3301** is equalto **845145127**, which gave us **http://845145127.com**. Note that 845145127 is also in brackets in the GPG key's name.

Going to this website led to an image of a cicada and a countdown. As the first puzzle ended within a month the following website won't work now.

Using OutGuess on the image produced the following message:

-----BEGIN PGP SIGNED MESSAGE-----
Hash: SHA1

You have done well to come this far.

Patience is a virtue.

Check back at 17:00 on Monday, 9 January 2012 UTC.

3301
-----BEGIN PGP SIGNATURE-----
Version: GnuPG v1.4.11 (GNU/Linux)

iQIcBAEBAgAGBQJPCKDUAAoJEBgfAeV6NQkPf9kP/19tbTFEy
+ol/vaSJ97A549+
E713DyFAuxJMh2AY2y5ksiqDRJdACBdvVNJqlaKHKTfihiY-
W75VHb+RuAbMhM2nN

C78eh+xd6c4UCwpQ9vSU4i1Jzn6+T74pMKkhyssaH-
hQWfPs8K7eKQxOJzSjpDFCS
FG7oHx6doPEk/xgLaJRCt/IJjNCZ9l2kYinmOm7c0QdRqJ+Vb-
V7Px41tP1dITQIH
/+JnETExUzWbE9fMf/eJl/zACF+gYii7d9Z-
dU8RHGi14jA2pRjc7SQArwqJOIyKQ
IFrW7zuicCYYT/GDmVSyILM03VXkNyAMBhG90edm17sx-
liyS0pA06MeOCjhDGUIw
QzBwsSZQJUsMJcXEUOpHPWrduP/zN5qHp/uUNNGj3vxLrnB
+wcjhF8ZOiDF6zk7+
ZVkdjk8dAYQr62EsEpfxMT2dv5bJ0YBaQGZHyjTEYnkiukZiD-
fExQZM2/uqhYOj3
yK0J+kJNt7QvZQM2enMV7jbaLTfU3VZGqJ6TSPqsfeiuGyx-
tlGLgJvd6kmiZkBB8
Jj0Rgx/h9Tc4m9xnVQanaPqbGQN4vZF3kOp/jAN5YjsRfCD-
b7iGvuEcFh4oRgpaB
3D2/+Qo9i3+CdAq1LMeM4WgCcYj2K5mtL0QhpNoeJ/
sOKzwnXA+mxBKoZ0S8dUX/
ZXCkbOLoMWCUfqBn8QkQ
=zn1y
-----END PGP SIGNATURE-----

At that time solvers waited. And waited. And waited. And finally, the website changed.

Reapplying OutGuess on the cicada image produced a new message, containing co-ordinates, as well as two which were written on the website itself:

52.216802, 21.018334
48.85057059876962, 2.406892329454422
48.85030144151387, 2.407538741827011
47.664196, -122.313301
47.637520, -122.346277
47.622993, -122.312576
37.5196666666667, 126.995
33.966808, -117.650488
29.909098706850486 -89.99312818050384
25.684702, -80.441289
21.584069, -158.104211
-33.90281, 151.18421
36.0665472222222, -94.1726416666667
37.577070, 126.813122

The coordinates pointed to locations around the globe.
14 locations in five different countries. At each location, there
was a poster with the cicada symbol and a QR code.

Warsaw, Poland

Paris, France

Sydney, Australia

Seoul, South Korea

Miami, FL, USA

The codes linked to an image

http://845145127.com/162667212858.jpg

The image contained two text files.

1

-----BEGIN PGP SIGNED MESSAGE-----
Hash: SHA1

**In twenty-nine volumes, knowledge was once contained.
How many lines of the code remained when the Mabinogion
paused?
Go that far in from the beginning and find my first name.**

1:29
6:46
the product of the first two primes
2:37
14:41
17:3
27:40
the first prime
2:33
1:1
7:45
17:29
21:31
12:17
the product of the first two primes
22:42
15:18
24:33
27:46
12:29
25:66
7:47

You've shared too much to this point. We want the best, not the followers. Thus, the first few there will receive the prize.

Good luck.

3301
-----BEGIN PGP SIGNATURE-----
Version: GnuPG v1.4.11 (GNU/Linux)

iQIcBAEBAgAGBQJPB1luAAoJEBgfAeV6NQkP9oAP+gLu+FsRD-
f3aRcJtBkCOU2MX

r/dagOTvCKWtuV+fedy0enWUZ+CbUjXOr98m9eq2z4iEG-
qKd3/MBXa+DM9f6YGUE
jPum4wHtQDSJlZMazuYqJOVZGw5XmF25+9mRM6fe3H9R-
CiNDZpuXl3MzwdivYhcG
B5hW14PcdHHteQf3eAUz+p+sO6RDs+q1sNGa/
rMQIx9QRe71EJwLMMkMfs81kfJC
tCt21+8ud0Xup4tjUBwul7QCcH9bqKG7cnR1XWsDgdF-
P6a4x9Jl2/IUvp1cfeT7B
YLS9W3lCM8thMemJr+ztQPZrpDlaLIitAT2L0B3f/
k4co89v5X2I/toY8Z3Cdvoi
hk0AdWzMy/XLDgkPnpEef/aFmnls53mqqe9xKAUQPMrI73hiJ
+5UZWuJdzCpvt+F
BjfQk15EJoUUW16K2+mBA1cSd+HJlnkslUTsjkq0E36XKChP
+Cvbu/p6DLUMM2Xl
+n3iospCkkHR9QDcHzE4Rxg9A435yHqqJ/sL2MXG/
CY8X4ec6U0/+UCIF9spuv8Y
7w66D05pI2u9M/081L7Br0i0Mpdf9fDblO/6GksskccaPkMQ3M-
RtsL+p9o6Dnbir
6Z2wH2Kw1Bf0Gfx4VcpHBikoWJ5blCc6tfvT+qXjVOZjWAL7D-
vReavSEmW1/fubN
C3RWcjeI4QET2oKmV2NK
=LWeJ
-----END PGP SIGNATURE-----

2

-----BEGIN PGP SIGNED MESSAGE-----
Hash: SHA1

A poem of fading death, named for a king
Meant to be read only once and vanish
Alas, it could not remain unseen.

1:5
152:24
the product of the first two primes
14:13
7:36
12:10
7:16
24:3
271:22
10:7
13:28
12:7
86:17
93:14
the product of the first two primes
16:7
96:4
19:13
47:2
71:22
75:9
77:4

You've shared too much to this point. We want the best, not the followers. Thus, the first few there will receive the prize.

Good luck.

3301
-----BEGIN PGP SIGNATURE-----
Version: GnuPG v1.4.11 (GNU/Linux)

iQIcBAEBAgAGBQJPB/nmAAoJEBgfAeV6NQkPEnEQAKl5qt-
b3ZE5vs+cO8KuzAi4a

tQEE71fvb65KQcX+PP5nHKGoLd0sQrZJw1c4VpMEg-
g9V27LSFQQ+3jSSyan7aIIg
SDqhmuAcliKwf5ELvHM3TQdyNb/OnL3R6UvavhfqdQwBXCD-
C9F0lwrPBu52MJqkA
ns93Q3zxec7kTrwKE6Gs3TDzjlu39YklwqzYcU-
SEusVzD07OVzhIEimsOVY+mW/C
X87vgXSlkQ69uN1XAZYp2ps8zl4LxoaBl5aVtIOA
+T8ap439tTBToov19nOerusB
6VHS192m5NotfQLnuVT4EITfloTWYD6X7RfqspGt1ft-
b1q6Ub8Wt6qCIo6eqb9xm
q2uVzbRWu05b0izAXkHuqkHWV3vwuSfK7cZQryYA7pUn-
akhlpCHo3sjIkh1FPfDc
xRjWfnou7TevkmDqkfSxwHwP5IKo3r5KB87c7i0/tOPuQTq-
WRwCwcWOWMNOS7ivY
KQkoEYNmqD2Yz3Esymjt46M3rAuazxk/gGYUmgHImgcu1zz-
K7Aq/IozXI7EFdNdu
3EoRJ/UL9Y0l0/PJOG5urdeeTyE0b8bwgfC2Nk/c8ebaTkFbOn-
zXdAvKHB03KEeU
PtM6d6DngL/LnUPFhmSW7K0REMKv62h9KyP/sw5QHTNh7Pz
+C63OO3BsFw+ZBdXL
hGqP6XptyZBsKvz2TLoX
=aXFt
-----END PGP SIGNATURE-----

A riddle. The solvers knew to be book codes along with a description of each book. They also included a warning in 1st file about too much collaboration, saying that only the first few, or the active few, that make it to the end will receive entry.

The second file led to a book.

Agrippa (A Book of the Dead)

The book led to a website with the help of the same decoding method used previously.

sq6wmgv2zcsrix6t.onion

A dark web website. Which most will know to be a hidden service on the Tor network. By entering this page into a tor-equipped browser, users found the following message:

Congratulations!

Please create a new email address with a public, free web-based service. Once you've never used before, and enter it below. We recommend you do this while still using tor, for anonymity.

We will email you a number within the next few days (in the order in which you arrived at this page). Once you've recieved it, come back to this page and append a slash and then the number you recieved to this url. (For example, if you recieved "3894894230934209", then you would go to "[http://

http://sq6wmgv2zcsrix6t.onion/3894894230934209]")

3301

but here the puzzle took an unexpected turn only a select group of first arrivals to this website were accepted into the final stage of the puzzle the site eventually closed down with a message :

We want the best, not the followers.

The finalists were also warned not to collaborate with others nor to share the details of this private stage of the puzzle. Well, given that we know this it's safe to say that not everyone heeded that warning but those who did presumably advanced through the final stages before reaching the very end of the possible.

Conclusion

Soon there was a month of silence and then this image was posted on the subreddit on Cicada.

Hello.

We have now found the individuals we sought.
Thus our month-long journey ends.

For now.

Thank you for your dedication and effort. If you were unable to complete the test, or did not receive an email, do not despair.

There will be more opportunities like this one.

Thank you all.

3301

P.S. 10412790658919985359827898739594318956404\
4425106955675643739226952372682423852959081734\
98343903703744757648634152034234993571087136314

According to the Cicada they have found the people they were looking for. But the community out there was not satisfied because of the lack of ending to what was this all about. And many termed it as a wild goose chase and waste of time. But did we know, this was just the beginning?

Theory of a user on subreddit claims he might have a clue.

In twenty-nine volumes, knowledge was once contained. How many lines of the code remained when the Mabinogian paused? Go that fair in from the beginning and find my last name." So I went and I searched for a Mabinogian.pdf, downloaded it, and did a highlight search for pause. At about line 255 with around 1242 lines left, might be different in translation, there was the word pause. So when you subtract 255 from 1242 you get 987. From here I went to the first sentence 29 volume book which stored knowledge. This is an encyclopedia. I then went to my bookshelf and opened up the A volume. What then happens took me a good 10–15 minutes to do, and that was count every individual line from A. At line 987 the word is Arthur. Meaning the writers name is Arthur. This is interesting for a few reasons. 1. Arthur mentions King Arthur a few times a few clues back. 2. In context of the Mabinogion the king is the one who pauses. 3. This means the person that wrote has a god complex.

The guy's name is Arthur unless you can prove otherwise.

"I'm not kidding. You can't make this s__t up"

◆ ◆ ◆

CRACKING THE CODE - 2013

On January 5th, 2013 exactly a year and a day after the first provoked this image was posted on 4chan.

Hello again. Our search for intelligent individuals now continues.

The first clue is hidden within this image.

Find it, and it will lead you on the road to finding us. We look forward to meeting the few that will make it all the way through.

Good luck.

3301

After a year of lackluster imitations, Cicada was back and it was time for round two.
The second puzzle was not too dissimilar from the first. Almost all decoding methods are the same.

The image enclosed a message

-----BEGIN PGP SIGNED MESSAGE-----
Hash: SHA1

Welcome again.

Here is a book code. To find the book, break this riddle:

A book whose study is forbidden
Once dictated to a beast;
To be read once and then destroyed
Or you shall have no peace.

I:1:6
I:2:15
I:3:26
I:5:4
I:6:15
I:10:26
I:14:136
I:15:68
I:16:42
I:18:17
I:19:14
I:20:58
I:21:10
I:22:8

I:23:6
I:25:17
I:26:33
I:27:30
I:46:32
I:47:53
I:49:209
I:50:10
I:51:115
I:52:39
I:53:4
I:62:43
I:63:8
III:19:84
III:20:10
III:21:11
III:22:3
III:23:58
5
I:1:3
I:2:15
I:3:6
I:14:17
I:30:68
I:60:11
II:49:84
II:50:50
II:64:104
II:76:3
II:76:3
0
I:60:11

Good luck.
3301

-----BEGIN PGP SIGNATURE-----
Version: GnuPG v1.4.11 (GNU/Linux)

iQIcBAEBAgAGBQJQ5QoZAAoJEBgfAeV6NQkPf2IQAK-
WgwI5EC33Hzje+YfeaLf6m
sLKjpc2Go98BWGReikDLS4PpkjX962L4Q3TZyzGenjJ-
SUAEcyoHVINbqvK1sMvE5
9lBPmsdBMDPreA8oAZ3cbwtI3QuOFi3tY2qI5sJ7GSfU-
giuI6FVVYTU/iXhXbHtL
boY4Sql5y7GaZ65cmH0eA6/418d9KL3Qq3qkTcM/tRA-
HhOZFMZfT42nsbcvZ2sWi
YyrAT5C+gs53YhODxEY0T9M2fam5AgUI-
WrMQa3oTRHSoNAefrDuOE7YtPy40j7kk
5/5RztmAzeEdRd8QS1ktHMezXEhdDP/
DEdIJCLT5eA27VnTY4+x1Ag9tsDFuitY4
2kEaVtCrf/36JAAwEcwOg2B/stdjXe1ORHFStY0N9wQ-
dReW3yAOBohvtOubicbYY
mSCS1Bx91z7uYOo2QwtRaxNs69beSSy+oWBef4u-
Tir8Q6WmgJpmzgmeG7ttEHquj
69CLSOWOm6Yc6qixsZy7ZkYDrSVrPwpAZ-
dEXip7OHST5QE/Rd1M8RWCOODba16Lu
URKvgl0/nZumrPQYbB1roxAaCMtlMoIOvwcyl-
dO0iOQ/2iD4Y0L4sTL7ojq2UYwX
bCotrhYv1srzBIOh+8vuBhV9ROnf/gab4tJII063EmztkBJ
+HLfstOqZFAPHQG22
41kaNgYIYeikTrweFqSK
=Ybd6
-----END PGP SIGNATURE-----

This led to a book.

From this book, a link is produced.

https:--www.dropbox.com-s-r7sgeb5dtmzj14s-3301

This came up with a 130MB hyperlink which leads to a .iso image. There were three directories, "data", "boot" and "audio".

2	3	5	7	11	13	17	19	23	29
31	37	41	43	47	53	59	61	67	71
73	79	83	89	97	101	103	107	109	113
127	131	137	139	149	151	157	163	167	173
179	181	191	193	197	199	211	223	227	229
233	239	241	251	257	263	269	271	277	281
283	293	307	311	313	317	331	337	347	349
353	359	367	373	379	383	389	397	401	409
419	421	431	433	439	443	449	457	461	463
467	479	487	491	499	503	509	521	523	541
547	557	563	569	571	577	587	593	599	601
607	613	617	619	631	641	643	647	653	659
661	673	677	683	691	701	709	719	727	733
739	743	751	757	761	769	773	787	797	809
811	821	823							

Screenshot from the video showing the prime number sequence being printed.

When booting from the image, a boot sequence appeared, printing a sequence of numbers to the screen. Investigating the sequence revealed that the live image prints out all prime numbers up to 3301. There were temporary two-second pauses at 1033 and 3301, where it stops at the latter and moves to the second stage. The next, and last stage of the procedure is a screen that reads:

@1231507051321
The key is all around you.

Good luck.
3301

Gradually the puzzle unfolded. The recording title uncovered.

The Instar Emergence.

Somebody found a twitter account through decoding the image deeply.

@1231507051321

(Note : 1231507051321 is a palindromic prime number)

This account led to an image.

Gematria Primus
an order and a value as revealed through 3301

Rune	Letter	Value	Rune	Letter	Value
ᚠ	F	2	ᛋ	S/Z	53
ᚢ	U	3	↑	T	59
ᚦ	TH	5	ᛒ	B	61
ᚩ	O	7	ᛗ	E	67
ᚱ	R	11	ᛗ	M	71
ᛣ	C/K	13	ᛚ	L	73
ᚷ	G	17	ᛝ	NG/ING	79
ᚹ	W	19	ᚫ	OE	83
ᚻ	H	23	ᛞ	D	89
ᚾ	N	29	ᚨ	A	97
ᛁ	I	31	ᚪ	AE	101
ᛄ	J	37	ᛘ	Y	103
ᛇ	EO	41	ᛡ	IA/IO	107
ᛈ	P	43	ᛉ	EA	109
ᛉ	X	47			

The image proved vital to the progression of the puzzle but the inclusion of the runic alphabets would remain a mystery for quite some time.

Much like the first puzzle, the second swelled into the physical world when a list of coordinates compelled participants to once again take to the streets in search of enigmatic posters.
This time it was 8 locations in four different countries.

Moscow, Russia

Columbus, USA

Okinawa, Japan

Little Rock, AR, USA

Each poster had a phone number on it as well as an access code. Note that each phone number either ends in 3301 or 1033.

Calling the phone number gave an automated speech asking for a code to be typed into the dialer. Solvers soon realized that they had to convert the access code given in the poster to its gentrified format and type that in. Upon doing so the following message was given (it varied depending on location, this one was for Portland):

Dataset:13
Offset:12821

Data:28C07E1B102D4D5C4C1A376E064477E1416FC C94928765

The data provided the user with a string of text, notably in this case "gbyh7znm6c7ezsmr.onion". It's important to note that each location gave a different onion address. All in all, 6 of the locations had their codes recovered, while the seventh was not physically visited, but the phone number obtained by wardialing all numbers ending in 1033.

Eventually, due to lack of leads, the trail went cold once again. Another select group of first arrivals have been accepted into a final private stage of the puzzle.

Conclusion

Unlike the first puzzle the second did not conclude with an official message from Cicada on any site. The trail merely went cold and cicada vanished once more leaving us no closer to an explanation.

However, this was still not the end

CRACKING THE CODE - 2014

At the beginning of 2014, on January 6th, 2014 on it was time for round three.

The Twitter account used by Cicada in 2013's puzzle was re-examined; after being inactive for about a year, it suddenly tweeted a link to an image on imgur.

Hello.

Epiphany is upon you. Your pilgrimage has begun. Enlightenment awaits.

Good luck.

3301

The image enclosed a message using OutGuess

-----BEGIN PGP SIGNED MESSAGE-----
Hash: SHA1

The work of a private man
who wished to transcend,
He trusted himself,
to produce from within.

1:2:3:1
3:3:13:5
45:5:2:3
20:3:20:5
8:3:8:6
48:5:14:2
21:13:4:1
25:1:7:4
15:9:3:4
1:1:16:3
4:3:3:1
8:3:26:4
47:3:3:5
3
13:2:5:4
1:4:16:4

.

o

n

i

o

n

Good luck.

3301

-----BEGIN PGP SIGNATURE-----

Version: GnuPG v1.4.11 (GNU/Linux)

iQIcBAEBAgAGBQJSyjguAAoJEBgfAeV6NQkPsgAP/A3t-
MC3lpyFNAc/sj+Izu15S
CzUjZJMe20Gu9UMNokQ2UJabktv9w0GMyK17TrM-
kUcU+ZpjdzGNqKoE2ETVxLmD/
uBZtR5PnF9EE3DO8tJUPN1vSrYNkYk+9zcaUJZMPNg-
YNCt/CACutPwrOci9i9FDO
7BIpnhGqT3ZruqrSwO2Y73LJI1xxUt1XUqh1NQ+fJeAF-
MRkJBZZazkxRlgk3GGsF
fLrcEKrS+KBipV1EQaaKxjISc9hc2c1TfxE66evlkN+zL-
coyDcYuyruNM5wiZzgM
2uR58c+xgWQgG5UuLFClfvjDxUvDkrKt4mzEeaY-
SUm1MsYueuYklz4ydlg5Mf6l2
p1WyAxO52XfXVUZASk6VmaEQ0WjODTXvLeFTxUS-
DoKDMkvxDVxX6wGkufS9JwakB
nTZizZ8Ypv8GcNCuNNGd6gZ1Vk2MYntggXdX8IN-
d0Itcd3QnLqbBnATDOinDxlOs
5zTrtyTHNaxxDagPfAbU1jMXM0aHd7PFAzjjp7kg-
CTWqMyBch+8Vt80bjkdL9iw8
Q3hxuanq8mh6nUGc+tNe0UfqKHEbE+jWIezYq-
gawJBOM9R5OhxWE+E+jPXtZKkXQ
JHYndPDrrsV8q27b7pOKN0+oblTkjqsItIAu-
Lu7FNdOB4xb1jjp1Sbh7WJdZ/rbi
mCOOvN/obU9qK1VfapyO
=6Gxk
-----END PGP SIGNATURE-----

The message led to a book

DOVER · THRIFT · EDITIONS

Ralph Waldo Emerson

SELF-RELIANCE
and Other Essays

The book produced a link

auqgnxjtvdbll3pv.onion

This led to yet another book which was mentioned in the fourth chapter

Liber Primus

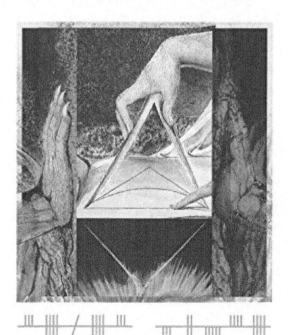

However, a significant portion of the book has yet to be translated. The Roenick text on some of the pages appears to be obfuscated by layers of encryption that has yet to be decrypted. After 74 pages featuring runes, only 19 have been successfully translated.

Third puzzle's leads are eventually onion links producing from Liber Primus pages. Solvers were submitting there leads to Cicada through onion hidden services. Onion links were going online and offline as per the submissions by solvers.

So far Third Puzzle and Liber Primus findings are as follows:

Onion 1

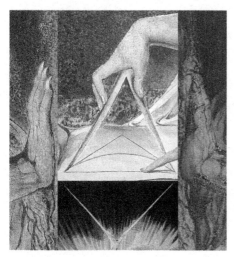

The William Blake Collage

Onion 2

634292ba49fe336edada779a34054a335c2ec12c8bbae
d4b92dcc05efe98f76abffdc2389bdb9de2cf20c009acdc1
945ab095a52609a5c219afd5f3b3edf10fcb25950666d
fe8d8c433cd10c0b4c72efdfe12c6270d5cfde291f9cf0d
73cb1211140136e4057380c963d70c76948d9cf6775
960cf98fbafa435c44015c5959837a0f8d9f46e094f27
c5797b7f8ab49bf28fa674d2ad2f726e197839956921
dab29724cd48e1a81fc9
bab3565f7513e3e368cd0327b47cf595afebb78d6b5b-
ca92ba021cd6734f4362a0b341f359157173b53d49ea
5dff5889d2c9de6b0d7e8c615286ce596bfa83f50b6ee-
abd153aaf50cd75f39929ba11fb0f8e8d611442846

The Growing String - 512 characters

cu343l33nqaekrnw.onion

Onion 3

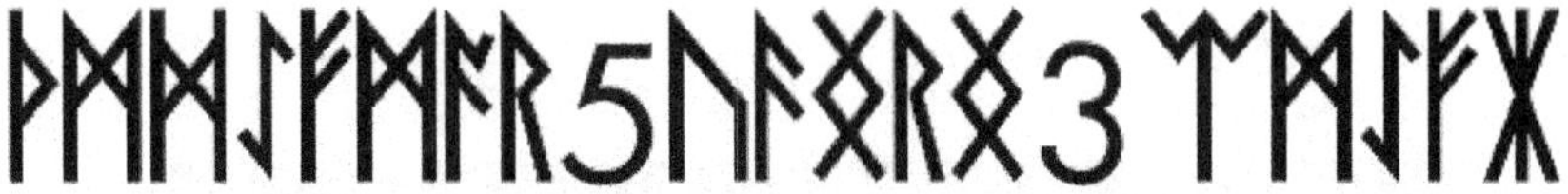

ᚦᛗᚻᛋ�miᛗᚨᚱ5ᚾᚨᚠᛟᚱᛟ3 ᛏᛈᛋᚠᚷ

Liber Primus Page 6 finding

Onion 4

avowyfgl5lkzfj3nonion
ᚦᛗᚻᛋᛈᚨᚱ5ᚾᚨᚠᛟᚱᛟ3 ᛏᛈᛋᚠᚷ

avowyfgl5lkzfj3n.onion

Onion 5

ut3qtzbrvs7dtvzp.onion

Onion 6

Magic Square

1033 Magic Square

| 1033 | 1033 | 1033 | 1033 | 1033 | 1033 | 1033 |

1033 = 272 + 138 + 341 + 131 + 151 = 1033

1033 = 366 + 199 + 130 + 320 + 18 = 1033

1033 = 226 + 245 + 91 + 245 + 226 = 1033

1033 = 18 + 320 + 130 + 199 + 366 = 1033

1033 = 151 + 131 + 341 + 138 + 272 = 1033

| 1033 | 1033 | 1033 | 1033 | 1033 | 1033 | 1033 |

ut3qtzbrvs7dtvzp.onion (Incomplete)

The End?
As usual, after the final submission, we heard nothing. The onions all went offline.

Long after the community as a whole had given up, a response was finally received. Some claim that they received emails from Cicada, and some claim they got a link to an onion, containing the remaining pages of the Liber Primus, a 58-page dump of images.

THE QUESTIONS

What About The Winners?

A good handful of people passed the test. They are still trying to find out what Cicada is and why they are searching for certain individuals. One of these winners goes by the name of Nox Populi.

He was a winner with the 2013 Cicada puzzle and still actively works on the subject. He has a YouTube channel consisting of tutorials for those who want to learn more about Cicada or those who are interested in learning the steps they need to take for future puzzles. He is very engaged with the community and even meets fans at conventions to talk about his experiences.

Joel Eriksson was another winner, one of the few who completed the 2012 Cicada puzzle. Like the others, he was a bit lost when Cicada left in silence after the completion of the puzzle. Eriksson was a cryptosecurity researcher and developer from Sweden.

In a 2015 interview with Rolling Stone, two alleged winners (Marcus Wanner and one other) of the first puzzle chronicled the events beyond the final stage after receiving an email from Cicada, they were taken to a forum on the dark web where they could communicate with 20 some-odd recruits as well as a handful of established members of Cicada. They were told that cicada 3301 had been founded by a group of friends who shared common ideals about security privacy and censorship the goal was to work as a collective to develop software applications in line with an ideology.

Later in 2012, the site was gone and they never heard from Cicada again.

What About The Unsolved Pages?

Unfortunately, some pages remain unsolved. But with the clues we have and the book unfinished, there is still time to figure this out once and for all. Those who do their part in the community and try to decode the book take us one step closer to identifying Cicada.

Let's just hope we find out soon.

Why Silence? Where Did They Go?

Cicada was famous for popping up with new puzzles every year, although they haven't come back in 2019 as of this writing. There didn't seem to be anything published in 2015, either. No one knows if Cicada has a headquarters or how long they have existed. At least one person claimed to be a part of Cicada for more than a decade.

Some people believe that when Cicada disappears, they are prepping recruits and new puzzles for a later time of completion. They may also be finishing up projects they have left in the past. Project CAKES could be an example.

According to Marcus, who had successfully completed the puzzles in 2012, his group had been collaborating on a project named CAKES through a website constructed by Cicada 3301. CAKES was created to protect whistle-blowers from retribution. But the project was dropped soon.

We don't know why it was started in the first place. We don't know who were they, some theorize that Cicada could be a secret group like the Illuminati.
We don't know the current status of the third puzzle, and the possibility of a fourth remains clouded in mystery.

ABOUT THE AUTHOR

Bhavesh Tekwani took full advantage of the long weekend and wrote his first case study book 'Unveiling Cicada 3301 - An Internet Mystery'. He is a passionate writer and an active content creator.

Find out more at his Amazon Author Page.

Or visit his social media handles:

Instagram - centrapublishing

Facebook - centrapublishing

Twitter - centrabooks

Can I Ask A Favour?

If you enjoyed this book, found it useful or otherwise then I'd really appreciate it if you would post a short review on Amazon. I do read all the reviews personally so that I can continually write what people are wanting.

If you'd like to leave a review then please visit the link below:

https://www.amazon.com/dp/B081BB8ZD8/ref=sr_1_5?
crid=1X0NWENGP8F3N&keywords=cicada
+3301&qid=1573533374&sprefix=cicada+3301%2Caps
%2C418&sr=8-5

Thanks for your support!

Mail - Centrapublishing@gmail.com

Made in the USA
Monee, IL
10 January 2021

57005877R00075